POINT PIÑOS LIGHT

The West Coast's Oldest Continuously Active Lighthouse

AILEEN WEINTRAUB

The Rosen Publishing Group's
PowerKids Press™
New York

To the Spivaks for being such shining lights, and for the best Shabbos tofu ever

Thanks also to our consultant Jerry McCaffery, author of Lighthouse, Point Piños

Published in 2003 by The Rosen Publishing Group, Inc.
29 East 21st Street, New York, NY 10010

Copyright © 2003 by The Rosen Publishing Group, Inc.

First Edition

Editors: Leslie Kaplan and Jennifer Landau
Book Design: Maria E. Melendez

Weintraub, Aileen, 1973–
        Point Piños Light : the West Coast's oldest continuously active lighthouse / Aileen Weintraub.
            p. cm. — (Great lighthouses of North America)
        Includes bibliographical references and index.
        Summary: This book provides a history of the Point Piños Light, the West Coast's oldest continuously operating lighthouse, completed in 1855.
            ISBN 0-8239-6173-7 (lib.)
            1. Point Piños Light (Pacific Grove, Calif.)—Juvenile literature   [1. Point Piños Light (Pacific Grove, Calif.)   2. Lighthouses]
I. Title   II. Series
        VK1025.P63 W45 2003   2001-003900
        387.1'55'0979476—dc21

Contents

This is an aerial view of Point Piños Light.
An aerial view is one that is taken from the air.

The Rocky Coast

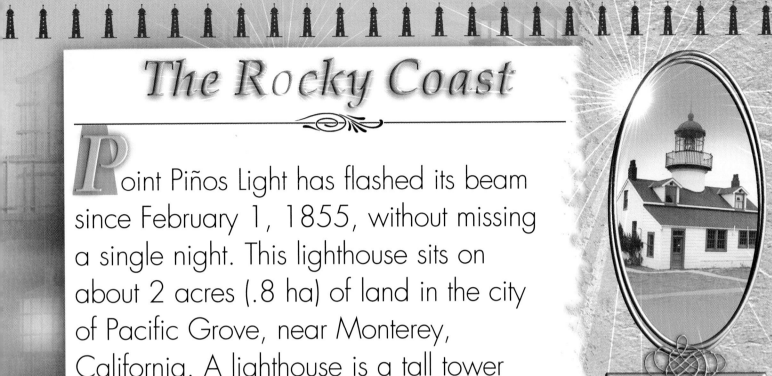

Point Piños Light has flashed its beam since February 1, 1855, without missing a single night. This lighthouse sits on about 2 acres (.8 ha) of land in the city of Pacific Grove, near Monterey, California. A lighthouse is a tall tower with a bright light at the top. This light helps to guide ships through the dark night. If a ship can't see where it's going, it might crash into rocks and sink. Both people and **cargo** could be lost. This happened many times on the rocky California coast. Point Piños Light is famous for being the oldest continuously active lighthouse on the West Coast. Alcatraz Island Light was built before it but wasn't always in use.

For more than a century, Point Piños Light (above) has helped to prevent shipwrecks.

5

Point of Pines

Sebastian Vizcaino was a famous Spanish explorer. In 1602, while sailing along what would one day be called the California coast, he came across a wooded area. He noticed the many pine trees growing in these woods. Vizcaino named the area Punta de los Piños, meaning "point of the pines" in Spanish. This is how Point Piños got its name. Years later, in 1850, the United States took control of California, including Punta de los Piños. Ship traffic increased along the West Coast. The **gold rush** had started, and people flocked to the area seeking their fortune. Ships full of expensive goods sailed to California for trade. With so many people going to the West Coast during the mid-1800s, a need grew for safer **navigation**. Merchants asked the government to make the dangerous California coastline safer for their ships.

In the 1840s, the gold rush drew thousands of people westward by route of the Oregon Trail. They rode in wagon trains like the one pictured above.

Point Piños Light still rests on the site chosen by its contractor, or the person hired to build the lighthouse.

Construction Begins

In the early 1850s, the U.S. government ordered eight lighthouses to be built along the West Coast. Three sites were picked as possibilities for the lighthouse that was to become Point Piños Light. The first site was rocky and was not a good place on which to build. The next site chosen was on solid ground but was too close to the ocean. A lighthouse built there could fall if waves washed away too much soil from its base. The third site was the farthest **inland** and the easiest for building. It was also a convenient location for getting stones with which to construct the lighthouse. Building so far inland meant that the light wouldn't reach as far out to sea. Still it would help to guide sailors. In 1853, the government sent workers on a ship called the *Oriole* to build the lighthouse. The ship carried wood, glass, and other supplies.

Cape Cod Style

At the top of a lighthouse is the lantern room, glassed-in housing for the lamp and the lens.

Point Piños Light was ready to guide ships to safety in 1855. This was the second lighthouse built on the West Coast. The lighthouse is called a Cape Cod–style house. This means that the tower rises up from the middle of the house. The house itself is one and a half stories high. The tower is made of brick, and the house is made of stone. The second floor of the house has two bedrooms separated by a **spiral** staircase that leads to the lantern room. The lantern room is where the light is kept. The tower itself is 43 feet (13 m) high. The light shines 89 feet (27 m) above the ground, because the tower is built on top of the house.

10

Inside Point Piños Light, newly redecorated rooms look similar to the way they did between 1893 and 1914.

The beauty of Point Piños Light is especially striking as the sun sets and the lighthouse glows against the evening sky.

Lighting the Tower

Point Piños Light uses a Fresnel lens to light the tower. A Frenchman named Augustin Fresnel invented the lens in 1822. This lens is shaped like a beehive. It is made of many pieces of glass. The glass on the top and the bottom of the beehive shape bends the light to bring it to a focus. The glass in the center **magnifies** the light. Together this sends out a thin, steady beam of light. The lenses come in six different sizes. A first **order** lens is the most powerful. Point Piños Light uses a third order Fresnel lens. The lighthouse was supposed to have a second order lens. Shipping for this lens was delayed, so a third order lens that was meant for use in another lighthouse was placed in Point Piños Light. This original lens is still in operation today.

Different Kinds of Light

The tower of Point Piños Light was first lit by whale oil. Electricity was turned on in the tower in 1919. Now the light comes from a 1,000-**watt** bulb. This bulb is 50,000 **candlepower**. One candlepower is the brightness of one candle.

Each lighthouse has its own **light signature**. This means that every lighthouse flashes in a unique way. Passing ships know which lighthouse they are near by looking at the light. When Point Piños Light was built, the light was a steady beam. In 1912, equipment was added to make the light flash. A falling weight caused a metal **shutter** to block the light for 10 seconds every 30 seconds. Today the light flashes 3 seconds on, 1 second off.

Point Piños's light can be seen for 17 miles (27 km) out to sea.

14

*The bright beam of Point Piños Light shines from the
lantern room at the top of the tower.*

Point Piños Light continues to operate as both a guide and a warning to ships sailing the rocky California coast.

Tending the Light

Today lighthouses are **automated**. This means that they run on their own, without keepers to tend the light. Point Piños Light was automated in 1975. Until then there was always one head keeper and at least one or two assistants tending the light. They took turns staying up at night to make sure the light worked properly. Before the use of electricity, keepers had to wind the gears that kept the shutter turning. This shutter was part of the equipment that made the light flash. Keepers had to keep the lens clean. They also had to watch closely for ships in danger. Keepers kept **logbooks** in which they recorded information such as the weather, descriptions of ships in need of help, and any unusual events at the lighthouse. When the night shift ended, keepers often cooked breakfast for the next person on duty.

17

Keepers at Point Piños

In their logbooks, keepers used to write with a quill, or feather, pen dipped in ink.

Most keepers were men, but there were female lighthouse keepers, too. Often if a keeper died, his wife took over the position. The first keeper at Point Piños Light was Charles Layton. He was killed in 1855, while trying to help catch a criminal in the area. His wife, Charlotte, took over as keeper at Point Piños Light. By that time, 30 female keepers had been operating lighthouses on the East Coast. Charlotte was the first female keeper on the West Coast. Many other women followed in her footsteps in the West. Charlotte remained the head keeper until 1860. That year she decided to marry her assistant, George Harris. After their marriage, he took over as head keeper.

The original Point Piños Light, in which the keepers lived, is still there today and can be visited by the public.

On the subject of the 1906 earthquake, keeper Emily Fish wrote in her logbook that first the animals started acting strangely, and then the ground began to shake.

Emily Fish

The most famous lighthouse keeper at Point Piños Light was Emily Fish. She was the wife of a well-to-do doctor. When he died, Emily decided to become a lighthouse keeper. She was called the **socialite** keeper, because she loved to entertain guests at the lighthouse. Emily served from 1893 to 1914. She decorated the house with **antiques** and kept the grounds full of plants and flowers. Her logbook records the earthquake of 1906. This is when the lighthouse tower cracked. The crack, which was repaired in 1906, did not stop the light from shining. Emily worked well into her old age, **retiring** at 71. She will be known forever as one of the most interesting female lighthouse keepers of all time.

Restoring Point Piños

Point Piños Light is run by the Pacific Grove Historical Society and the U.S. **Coast Guard**. The lighthouse has been **restored** to show different time periods throughout history. Many of the rooms have been restored to look as they did while Emily Fish lived there. One room is **dedicated** to World War II, when the tower was used to watch for enemy ships. Today the lighthouse is full of hands-on displays. These include a big bell for visitors to ring, and a foghorn they can sound. This lighthouse has been shining brightly every night since 1855. It serves as a great reminder of **maritime** history.

Point Piños Light has never missed a night of shining since it was first lit.

Glossary

antiques (an-TEEKS) Works of art or pieces of furniture made a long time ago.

automated (AW-tuh-mayt-ed) When something operates on its own without help.

candlepower (KAN-duhl-pow-uhr) The amount of light coming from one candle.

cargo (KAR-go) Goods on a ship.

coast guard (KOHST GARD) The part of the military that patrols the waters.

dedicated (DEH-dih-kay-tid) To have set apart for a special purpose.

gold rush (GOHLD RUSH) When people rush to an area where gold has been discovered. The discovery of gold in California in 1848 brought more than 40,000 people there within two years.

inland (IN-land) Away from the coast or the border.

light signature (LYT SIG-nuh-chur) The special way a lighthouse light flashes so it can be told apart from others.

logbooks (LAHG-buks) Books for keeping records.

magnifies (MAG-nih-fyz) Causes light to appear stronger.

maritime (MAR-ih-tym) Having to do with the sea.

navigation (nah-vuh-GAY-shun) A way of figuring out which way a ship is going.

order (OR-der) The size of the Fresnel lens that determines the brightness and the distance that light will travel.

restored (rih-STORD) When a building has had work done to it to make it look like it once did.

retiring (rih-TY-ring) Giving up one's job.

shutter (SHUH-ter) A movable cover for a window or a door.

socialite (SOH-sheh-lyt) A person who is very well known and important in society.

spiral (SPY-ruhl) Winding or circular.

watt (WAHT) A unit for measuring electric power.

Index

Web Sites

To learn more about Point Piños Light, check out these Web sites:

http://216.55.23.140/lighthouse/pinos.html
www.pgmuseum.org/Lighthouse.htm

24